HOMEWORK SURVIVAL GUIDE

Math

A REFERENCE FOR STUDENTS AND PARENTS

by Teri Crawford Jones

illustrated by Andrea Champlin

Troll

Copyright © 1998 by Troll Communications L.L.C.

Cover and interior pages designed by: Bob Filipowich

Developed and produced by: WWK Consulting Group, Inc., 201 West 70 Street, New York, NY 10023

Printed in the United States of America. ISBN 0-8167-4815-2

10 9 8 7 6 5 4 3 2 1

TABLE OF CONTENTS

Helping children do their homework successfully requires some planning. Study habits and time management are important skills for children to learn. The following tips may give you and your child strategies for doing homework more efficiently. Both you and your child will learn to survive Math homework!

- Have your child do homework immediately after coming home from school. A quick snack is okay, but any other activity should wait until later.

- Make sure your child has a quiet, well-lit place to work.

- Help your child gather the materials necessary for his or her homework. Remember to have enough pencils, paper, and other tools ready.

- Try to schedule after-school activities on days when there is not as much homework.

- Work carefully. It is easy to make mathematical errors when one works too quickly.

- Children need encouragement and reassurance. Patience and praise help children to become better students.

CHAPTER 1

What Are Numbers?

The number system we use—the decimal system—is based on the number 10 and has ten symbols: 0, 1, 2, 3, 4, 5, 6, 7, 8, 9. If you look at the number of fingers you have, you can guess how a base 10 system probably was developed. Even the word digit means both "finger" and "numeral."

Numbers come in different groups, or sets:

Counting numbers begin with 1 and continue with 2, 3, 4, 5, 6, 7, 8, 9, 10, and so on.

All counting numbers are whole numbers. However, whole numbers also include 0 (zero): 0, 1, 2, 3, 4, 5, 6, 7, 8, 9, 10, and so on.

A rational number is any number that can be written as a fraction, such as $\frac{4}{5}$. The only exception is that the bottom number, or denominator, cannot be equal to 0. (See page 21 for more information about fractions.)

A prime number can be divided evenly only by 1 and itself. For example, 7 can be divided evenly only by 7 and 1:

$$7 \div 7 = 1 \qquad 7 \div 1 = 7$$

A prime number has only two factors: 1 and itself. Factors are the numbers you multiply to find the product.

$$1 \times 7 = 7$$

The only two factors in this problem are 7 and 1.

What are the factors in the problem 1x2=2? Write your answers on the flap.

Can you list the remaining prime numbers to 100? Write your answers on the flap.

THE PRIME NUMBERS FROM 1 TO 50
2, 3, 5, 7, 11, 13, 17, 19, 23, 29, 31, 37, 41, 43, 47

Counting numbers that are not prime numbers are called **composite numbers**. These numbers have *more than* two factors. For example, 6 is a composite number because its factors are 1, 2, 3, and 6 (2 × 3 = 6, 1 × 6 = 6).

> ## THE COMPOSITE NUMBERS FROM 1 TO 50
>
> **4, 6, 8, 9, 10, 12, 14, 15, 16, 18, 20, 21, 22, 24, 25, 26, 27, 28, 30, 32, 33, 34, 35, 36, 38, 39, 40, 42, 44, 45, 46, 48, 49, 50**

List the composite numbers from 51 to 100. Write your answers on the flap.

The number 1 is neither prime nor composite. It has only one factor and can only be divided by itself.

Numbers are either **even** or **odd**. Even means a number can be divided equally by 2.

Odd means that a number cannot be divided equally by 2. Numbers that end with 0, 2, 4, 6, and 8 are even. Numbers that end with 1, 3, 5, 7, and 9 are odd.

Integers include both **positive whole numbers**, which are greater than 0, and their opposites, which are called **negative whole numbers**.

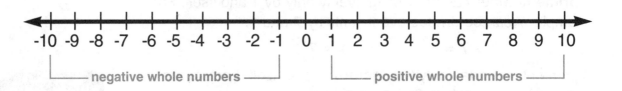

Absolute value is the distance a number is from 0. The symbol for absolute value is two slash marks: / /. The absolute value of a number is always written as a positive number. For example, if you see *I-5I* = **5**, you can read it as *the absolute value of negative 5 is 5*, because negative 5 is 5 places from 0.

PLACE VALUE

The **value** of a number depends on its **place**. For example, in the number 222, there are two hundreds, two tens, and two ones. Each place is ten times greater than the place to its right. You can see how this works in a **place-value chart**.

Hundreds	Tens	Ones
2	2	2

The three places in the chart make a **period**. Hundreds, tens, and ones are the **ones period**. To count periods, start from the ones place on the right. Each period in a number is separated by a comma. A place-value chart also helps you read larger numbers.

When you write numbers in groups of ten, **use zero** (0) **as a placeholder**.

Thousands	Hundreds	Tens	Ones
4 ,	0	0	0
4 thousands	no hundreds	no tens	no ones

Numbers can also be written in a form called **expanded notation**. This means the number is spread out, or "expanded," to show the place value of each digit. For example, **340,625,093** is written in **standard notation**. This is the number in expanded notation:

300,000,000 + 40,000,000 + 600,000 + 20,000 + 5,000 + 90 + 3

(three hundred forty million, six hundred twenty-five thousand, ninety-three)

Place value helps you **compare** and **order** numbers. For example, if you compare 37 and 73, you'll see that 73 is the greater number because it has 7 tens and 3 ones. The number 37 has only 3 tens.

Tens	Ones
3	7
7	3

How do you write 222,222,222,222 in expanded notation? How do you read this number? Write your answers on the flap.

SYMBOLS TO COMPARE NUMBERS

< is less than   ≤ is less than or equal to

> is greater than   ≥ is greater than or equal to

When you order more than two numbers, you compare the place value of each digit. To order the numbers 192, 143, and 41 from largest to smallest, compare the hundreds, the tens, and the ones.

Hundreds	Tens	Ones
1	9	2
1	4	3
	4	1

The hundreds digits are the same, so look at the tens. Nine is greater than 4, so 192 is the largest number. Forty-one has no hundreds, so 143 is the next-largest number. Forty-one is the smallest number.

Use a **rounded number** to estimate how many. To round to the nearest 10, round down to the lower ten if the ones digit is less than 5. If the ones digit is 5 or greater, round up to the next 10. For example, the number 324 can be rounded down to 320, while the number 687 can be rounded up to 690.

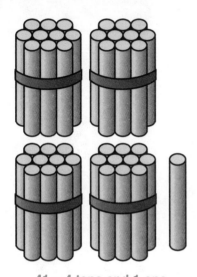

41 = 4 tens and 1 one

ROMAN NUMERALS

Before **Arabic numerals** were used, the ancient Romans used seven letters in different combinations to make numbers.

ROMAN NUMERALS

I = 1	D = 500	$\overline{L}$ = 50,000
V = 5	M = 1,000	$\overline{C}$ = 100,000
X = 10	$\overline{I}$ = 1,000	$\overline{D}$ = 500,000
L = 50	$\overline{V}$ = 5,000	$\overline{M}$ = 1,000,000
C = 100	$\overline{X}$ = 10,000	

> A bar over a letter means to multiply the value by 1,000.

> How do you write 16, 40, and 104 in Roman numerals? Write your answers on the flap.

When a letter of lesser value is placed to the *right* of a letter with greater value, add the two values.

VI = 6   XVII = 17

When a letter of lesser value is placed to the *left* of a letter with greater value, subtract the lesser value from the greater.

XXIX = 29   IV = 4

CHAPTER 2

Putting It Together

When you put two or more numbers together, you **add** them. When you take away one or more numbers from another number, you **subtract** them.

Addition

$12 + 11 = 23$

addends   sum

Subtraction

$17 - 9 = 8$

minuend   subtrahend   difference

A sentence can be written in symbols to show an **addition** or **subtraction fact**. This sentence is called an **equation**, and it has two parts that are separated by an **equal sign** (=).

REGROUPING

When two or more numbers added together equal more than 9, regroup the value that is 10 or more into the next place.

$$\begin{array}{r} 1\ 1\ 1 \\ 23{,}761 \\ +\ \ 8{,}496 \\ \hline 32{,}257 \end{array}$$

- 6 + 1 equals 7

- 60 + 90 equals 150. One hundred is regrouped to the hundreds place, leaving 5 tens in the tens place.

- 700 + 400 + 100 equals 1,200. Regrouping one thousand to the thousands place leaves 2 hundreds in the hundreds place.

- 3,000 + 8,000 + 1,000 equals 12,000. One ten thousand is regrouped to the ten thousands place, leaving 2 thousands in the thousands place.

- 20,000 + 10,000 equals 30,000 or 3 ten thousands.

Ten Thousands	Thousands	Hundreds	Tens	Ones
2^1	3^1	7^1	6	1
	8	4	9	6
3 ten thousands	2 thousands	2 hundreds	5 tens	7 ones

Keep track of the numbers by writing the regrouped number above the correct place. Then add the regrouped number to the other numbers in that place.

When you subtract, regroup if the minuend is smaller than the subtrahend.

$$\begin{array}{r} {}^{1}\,{}^{1} \\ 4\ \ 3 \\ 5\!\!\!\!/4\,3 \leftarrow \text{minuend} \\ -\ 267 \leftarrow \text{subtrahend} \\ \hline 276 \leftarrow \text{difference} \end{array}$$

- The minuend in the ones place (3) is smaller than the subtrahend in the ones place (7).
- One ten is regrouped to the ones place, leaving three tens in the tens place. $13 - 7$ equals 6.
- The new minuend in the tens place (30) is smaller than the subtrahend in the tens place (60).
- One hundred is regrouped to the tens place, leaving four hundreds in the hundreds place. $130 - 60$ equals 70.
- Subtract the subtrahend (200) from the new minuend in the hundreds place (400). $400 - 200$ equals 200.

Hundreds	Tens	Ones
$4\cancel{5}$	$\cancel{4}^{1}3$	$^{1}3$
$-\ 2$	6	7
2 hundreds	**7** tens	**6** ones

A. $\begin{array}{r} 346 \\ -\ 49 \\ \hline \end{array}$ **B.** $\begin{array}{r} 6{,}922 \\ +\ 8{,}579 \\ \hline \end{array}$ **C.** $\begin{array}{r} 14{,}816 \\ -\ 3{,}687 \\ \hline \end{array}$

ADDITION PROPERTIES

These special properties of addition help you add:

ADDITION PROPERTIES

Commutative: The order of the addends does not change the sum.

$$7 + 3 = 10 \qquad 3 + 7 = 10$$

Associative: The way the addends are grouped does not change the sum.

$$(3 + 2) + 5 = 3 + (2 + 5)$$

Identity: The sum of any number and zero is that number.

$$2{,}000 + 0 = 2{,}000$$

Can you compute these facts? Write your answers on the flap.

Since addition and subtraction are related, just reverse the operation to check your work.

Example: 65 - 38 = 27. To check, add 27 to 38. Your answer should be 65.

ESTIMATION

Before you add or subtract, **estimation** will give you an idea of what a reasonable answer should be.

There are two ways to estimate a sum.
Look at the examples below.

1. Add the first digits.

$$
\begin{array}{r}
4,689 \\
3,221 \\
+\ 5,129 \\
\hline
12,000 \ \text{estimate}
\end{array}
$$

Adjust the estimate by using the digits to the right of the first digits.

$$
\begin{array}{r}
4,689 \\
3,221 \quad \text{The hundreds digits add up to about 1,000.} \\
+\ 5,129 \\
\hline
12,000 + 1,000 = 13,000 \ \text{adjusted estimate}
\end{array}
$$

2. You can also round each number to estimate a sum.

$$
\begin{array}{rll}
4,689 & \text{rounds to} & 5,000 \\
3,221 & \text{rounds to} & 3,000 \\
+\ 5,129 & \text{rounds to} & +\ 5,000 \\
\hline
& & 13,000 \ \text{estimate}
\end{array}
$$

The exact answer, 13,039, is very close to the estimate!

To subtract, you can use the same rules of estimation.

A.
$$
\begin{array}{r}
9,875 \\
6,221 \\
+\ 4,365 \\
\hline
\end{array}
$$

B.
$$
\begin{array}{r}
11,246 \\
-\ 3,851 \\
\hline
\end{array}
$$

C.
$$
\begin{array}{r}
12,828 \\
-\ 5,179 \\
\hline
\end{array}
$$

D.
$$
\begin{array}{r}
3,687 \\
7,211 \\
+8,746 \\
\hline
\end{array}
$$

Estimate the answers to the problems at the left. Write your answers on the flap.

As explained on page 6, integers include both positive whole numbers, which are greater than 0, and their opposites, which are called negative whole numbers.

NOTES ABOUT INTEGERS

When you add negative numbers, the sum is less than either negative addend:

$$-7 + -2 = -9$$

Adding a negative number to a positive number is like subtracting the negative number from the positive.

$$7 + -2 = 5$$

Subtracting two negative numbers is like adding a positive number to a negative.

$$-7 - -2 = -5$$

When you subtract a larger positive number (7) from a smaller positive number (3), the answer is a negative number.

$$3 - 7 = -4$$

Can you complete these facts?
A. 12 + -8 = ?
B. -15 - -11 =?
Write your answers on the flap.

MAGIC SQUARES

In a magic square, the sums of every row, column, and diagonal are equal.

Look at the unfinished magic square on the right. Can you find the missing numbers? Write your answers on the flap.

3	4	2
2	3	4
4	2	3

The sum of this magic square is 9.

17	4		14
6	11	12	9
10		8	13
5	16	15	2

CHAPTER 3

To Multiply or Divide

Multiplication is a shortcut for combining numbers when you have equal groups to add. If you want to find the total number of baseball cards in a binder that has 6 pages and 8 cards on each page, you could add:

$$8 + 8 + 8 + 8 + 8 + 8 = 48$$

But it's faster to multiply:

$$6 \text{ (pages)} \times 8 \text{ (cards on each page)} = 48$$

In multiplication, you have **multipliers** and **multiplicands** instead of addends, and a **product** instead of a sum. A multiplication sentence is also called an **equation**.

$$
\begin{array}{l}
6 \leftarrow \text{multiplicand} \\
\underline{\times\ 8} \leftarrow \text{multiplier} \\
48 \leftarrow \text{product}
\end{array}
$$

MULTIPLICATION PROPERTIES

Commutative: The order in which numbers are multiplied does not change the product.

$$6 \times 8 = 48 \qquad 8 \times 6 = 48$$

Associative: The way in which numbers are grouped does not change the product.

$$
\begin{array}{ll}
(5 \times 2) \times 6 = 60 & 5 \times (2 \times 6) = 60 \\
10\ \ \times 6 = 60 & 5 \times\ \ 12\ \ = 60
\end{array}
$$

Identity: The product of 1 and any number is that number.

$$1 \times 8 = 8 \qquad 1 \times 1 = 1$$

Zero: The product of zero and any number is zero.

$$17 \times 0 = 0 \qquad 1 \times 0 = 0$$

There are many steps to multiplying large numbers.
Look at this example.

$$
\begin{array}{r}
\overset{1}{} \\
\overset{3\,5}{} \\
536 \\
\times\ 29 \\
\hline
4{,}824 \\
+10{,}720 \\
\hline
15{,}544
\end{array}
$$

A. Multiply the ones. Start with $9 \times 6 = 54$.

B. Write 4 ones. Regroup 5 tens to the tens column.

C. Multiply $9 \times 3 = 27$.

D. Add the 5 tens you regrouped: $27 + 5 = 32$.

E. Write 2 tens. Regroup 3 hundreds to the hundreds column.

F. Multiply $9 \times 5 = 45$.

G. Add the 3 hundreds you regrouped: $45 + 3 = 48$.

H. Write 48 hundreds. So, $9 \times 536 = 4{,}824$.

I. Write 0 as a placeholder in the ones place.

J. Multiply the tens: $2 \times 6 = 12$.

K. Write 2 tens in the tens column. Regroup 1 ten to the tens column.

L. Multiply $2 \times 3 = 6$.

M. Add the 1 ten you regrouped: $6 + 1 = 7$.

N. Write 7 hundreds in the hundreds column.

O. Multiply $2 \times 5 = 10$.

P. Write 10 thousands. So, $20 \times 536 = 10{,}720$.

Q. Add: $4{,}824 + 10{,}720 = 15{,}544$.

Use the same process to multiply money. Remember to bring down the decimal point to show cents and to write the dollar sign. (See pages 25-26 for more information about decimals.)

CDs $11.99

Find the product of the following problem.
$11.99 x 5 = ?
Write your answer on the flap.

Multiply problems A-C, and don't forget that 0 times any number is 0. Write your answers on the flap.

A. $\begin{array}{r} 43 \\ \times\ 34 \\ \hline \end{array}$

B. $\begin{array}{r} 406 \\ \times\ 58 \\ \hline \end{array}$

C. $\begin{array}{r} 8{,}094 \\ \times\ 54 \\ \hline \end{array}$

MULTIPLICATION FACTS

Knowing multiplication facts helps you multiply larger numbers using mental math.

MULTIPLICATION TABLE

X	0	1	2	3	4	5	6	7	8	9
1	0	1	2	3	4	5	6	7	8	9
2	0	2	4	6	8	10	12	14	16	18
3	0	3	6	9	12	15	18	21	24	27
4	0	4	8	12	16	20	24	28	32	36
5	0	5	10	15	20	25	30	35	40	45
6	0	6	12	18	24	30	36	42	48	54
7	0	7	14	21	28	35	42	49	56	63
8	0	8	16	24	32	40	48	56	64	72
9	0	9	18	27	36	45	54	63	72	81

Find the two numbers you want to multiply. Use your finger to follow across and down until they meet. That number is the product.

When you multiply one number by another number, the product is a **multiple** of each of the numbers.

Common multiples of two or more numbers are multiples that are shared by all the numbers. For example, 0, 18, 36, and 54 are common multiples of 6 and 9.

The **least common multiple**, known as the **LCM**, of two or more numbers is the lowest number, except 0, that is a multiple of all the numbers. For example, 18 is the least common multiple of 6 and 9.

What are two common multiples of 4 and 10? What is the least common multiple of 6 and 8? Write your answers on the flap.

15

FACTORS EXPONENTS

FACTORS

Numbers you multiply to find a product are also called **factors**.

The factors of 24 are 1, 2, 3, 4, 6, 8, 12, 24.

$$1 \times 24 = 24 \qquad 2 \times 12 = 24$$
$$3 \times 8 = 24 \qquad 4 \times 6 = 24$$

The **common factors** of two or more numbers are factors that are shared by all the numbers.

The **greatest common factor**, known as the **GCF**, of two or more numbers is the largest factor that is the same for all the numbers. For example, the GCF of 12 and 24 is 12.

A **composite number** is a whole number greater than 1 that has more than two factors. You can find the prime, or smallest, factors of a composite number by using a **factor tree**. Prime factors are always prime numbers.

Draw factor trees to find the prime factors of 30 and 44. Write your answers on the flap.

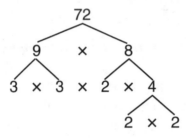

The prime factors of 72 are 3 and 2.

The prime factors of 38 are 2 and 19.

EXPONENTS

What would the product be for 5^4? Write your answer on the flap.

When one number is repeated as a factor in an equation ($4 \times 4 \times 4 \times 2 = 128$), use an **exponent** to shorten the equation ($4^3 \times 2 = 128$).

The number 4 is the **base** and 3 is the **exponent**, or the number of times the base number will be multiplied.

COMMON EXPONENTS

$1^2 = 1$	$3^2 = 9$	$5^2 = 25$	$7^2 = 49$	$9^2 = 81$
$2^2 = 4$	$4^2 = 16$	$6^2 = 36$	$8^2 = 64$	$10^2 = 100$

DIVISION

When you divide, you find out how many times a number fits into another number. The number 6 fits into the number 30 five times. Division can also be thought of as repeated subtraction of the same number.

$$30 - 6 - 6 - 6 - 6 - 6 = 0$$

The number 6 can be subtracted from 30 five times, or 30 can be divided by 6 five times.

Here are two ways to write a division sentence.

$$30 \div 6 = 5$$

dividend   divisor   quotient

$$6 \overline{)30}$$ ← quotient
← dividend

divisor

The divisor always goes on the outside of the division sign ($\overline{)}$).

There are many steps to dividing numbers. Look at this example.

$$
\begin{array}{r}
231 \\
42 \overline{)9702} \\
-84 \\
\hline
130 \\
-126 \\
\hline
42 \\
-42 \\
\hline
0
\end{array}
$$

A. How many times does 42 go into 97 hundreds? Think: 42 × 2 equals 84.

B. Write 2 hundreds in the hundreds place and multiply 2 × 42.

C. Subtract the product from the first two digits of the dividend. 97 − 84 equals 13.

D. Bring down the next digit in the dividend (0).

E. How many times does 42 go into 130 tens? Think: 42 × 3 equals 126.

F. Write three tens in the tens place and multiply 3 × 42.

G. Subtract the product from the dividend. 130 − 126 equals 4.

H. Bring down the next digit in the dividend (2).

I. How many times does 42 go into 42? (This is an easy one!)

J. Write 1 in the ones place and multiply 1 × 42.

K. Subtract the product from the dividend. 42 − 42 = 0.

L. Check your answer by multiplying. 231 × 42 equals 9,702.

Remember basic division facts, such as 42 ÷ 7 = 6, by thinking of the related multiplication fact, 6 × 7 = 42.

Solve this division problem.

752 ÷ 16 = ?

Write your answer on the flap.

RULES OF DIVISION

- A whole number divided by 1 is equal to itself.

$$56 \div 1 = 56$$

- 0 divided by a whole number is always 0.

$$0 \div 32 = 0$$

- A number cannot be divided by 0.

REMAINDERS

When a number does not divide evenly, the number left over is the **remainder**.

```
      173 R6
 7 )1,217
    − 7↓|
      51|
    − 49↓
      27
    − 21
       6
```

$$173 \times 7 = 1,211 + 6 = 1,217$$

Write the remainder next to the quotient. The letter "R" identifies the remainder.

A. 8,175 ÷ 7 = ?   **B.** 4,604 ÷ 6 = ?   **C.** 630 ÷ 70 = ?

Solve the division problems at the right. Write your answers on the flap.

DIVISION PATTERNS

Knowing basic division facts and looking for patterns of ten can help you divide larger numbers.

```
        3,600 ÷ 40 =   ?
If         36 ÷ 4  =   9
then      360 ÷ 4  =  90
          360 ÷ 40 =   9
        3,600 ÷ 40 =  90
```

To **estimate a quotient** when dividing by a divisor that has more than one digit, round the divisor first.

5,563 ÷ 84   Round the divisor (84) and dividend (5,563) to 80 and 5,600. 56 is evenly divisible by 8 (56 ÷ 8 = 7). So 5,600 ÷ 80 = 70.

Your estimate is about 70. The exact answer shows that the estimate is correct: 5,563 ÷ 84 = 66 R19.

ORDER OF OPERATIONS

Addition, subtraction, multiplication, and division are **operations**. Follow these rules when you have to do more than one operation.

ORDER OF OPERATIONS

1. Multiply and divide first. Then do any addition or subtraction.

$$(3 \times 4) + 7 = 12 + 7 = 19$$
$$\text{NOT}\quad 3 \times (4 + 7) = 3 \times 11 = 33$$

2. If several numbers are multiplied or divided in one expression, do the operations in the order in which they appear from left to right.

$$9 \div 3 \times 7 = (9 \div 3) \times 7 = 3 \times 7 = 21$$

3. When numbers are grouped in parentheses or have exponents, follow these steps:

- Do the operations inside parentheses.
- Do the work with exponents.
- Do the multiplication and division from left to right.
- Do the addition and subtraction from left to right.

$8 \times 3^2 + 5 \times (7+2) = ?$ **Step 1:** $7+2 = 9$

$8 \times 3^2 + 5 \times 9 = ?$ **Step 2:** $3^2 = 3 \times 3 = 9$

$8 \times 9 + 5 \times 9 = ?$ **Step 3:** $8 \times 9 = 72$

                                       $5 \times 9 = 45$

$72 + 45 = 117$ **Step 4:** $72+45 = 117$

Show the steps for the expression
$5 \times 4^3 + 16 + (5 + 3) = ?$
Write your answer on the flap.

SQUARES AND SQUARE ROOTS

SQUARES AND SQUARE ROOTS

When you multiply a number by itself, you **square** that number. For example, 2×2 is **2 squared** (2^2), which is equal to 4.

4 squared: $4^2 = 4 \times 4 = 16$ 5 squared: $5^2 = 5 \times 5 = 25$

This means that 4, 16, and 25 are all **square numbers**.

The **square root** of a square number (for example, 25) is the number that, multiplied by itself, results in the square number. The square root of 25 is 5.

The symbol for a square root is called a **radical sign** ($\sqrt{}$).

> Find the square root of 361. Write your answer on the flap.

SQUARE ROOT TABLE

$\sqrt{1} = 1$	$\sqrt{225} = 15$	$\sqrt{841} = 29$
$\sqrt{4} = 2$	$\sqrt{256} = 16$	$\sqrt{900} = 30$
$\sqrt{9} = 3$	$\sqrt{289} = 17$	$\sqrt{961} = 31$
$\sqrt{16} = 4$	$\sqrt{324} = 18$	$\sqrt{1024} = 32$
$\sqrt{25} = 5$	$\sqrt{361} = 19$	$\sqrt{1089} = 33$
$\sqrt{36} = 6$	$\sqrt{400} = 20$	$\sqrt{1156} = 34$
$\sqrt{49} = 7$	$\sqrt{441} = 21$	$\sqrt{1225} = 35$
$\sqrt{64} = 8$	$\sqrt{484} = 22$	$\sqrt{1296} = 36$
$\sqrt{81} = 9$	$\sqrt{529} = 23$	$\sqrt{1369} = 37$
$\sqrt{100} = 10$	$\sqrt{576} = 24$	$\sqrt{1444} = 38$
$\sqrt{121} = 11$	$\sqrt{625} = 25$	$\sqrt{1521} = 39$
$\sqrt{144} = 12$	$\sqrt{676} = 26$	$\sqrt{1600} = 40$
$\sqrt{169} = 13$	$\sqrt{729} = 27$	
$\sqrt{196} = 14$	$\sqrt{784} = 28$	

CHAPTER 4

The Big "D" Meets Action Fraction

FRACTIONS

A **fraction** is a part of a number and describes part of a whole. A fraction has two parts. The bottom number is the **denominator**. It tells how many parts there are in the whole. The **numerator** is the top number. It tells the number of parts of the denominator taken.

$$\frac{1 \longleftarrow \text{numerator}}{2 \longleftarrow \text{denominator}}$$

> The word fraction comes from a Latin word, fractio, which means "broken into pieces."

This fraction tells you that one part is counted out of the two parts in the whole.

A whole can be a **set** of things, such as the five animals above. $\frac{3}{5}$ of the animals in the set are dogs, and $\frac{2}{5}$ are cats.
You also can say 3 out of 5 animals are dogs, and 2 out of 5 animals are cats.

A whole can also be a **region** made up of parts. The square is separated into four parts, or fourths. $\frac{2}{4}$, or two parts, of the region are shaded. Or you could say that $\frac{1}{2}$ of the square is shaded, since $\frac{2}{4} = \frac{1}{2}$.

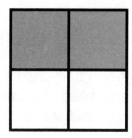

Notice that the larger the denominator, the smaller the fraction. This means that $\frac{1}{8}$ is a smaller part of a region or set than $\frac{1}{4}$.

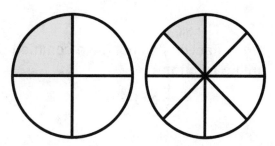

In a **proper fraction**, the numerator is smaller than the denominator. All proper fractions have a value that is less than one. **Improper fractions** are fractions that have a value equal to or greater than one. In an improper fraction, the numerator is the same as or greater than the denominator. For example:

$$\frac{5}{2} \qquad \frac{10}{3} \qquad \frac{9}{9}$$

Improper fractions greater than one can be written as mixed numbers. A **mixed number** includes a whole number and a fraction.

$$\frac{5}{2} = 2\frac{1}{2} \qquad \frac{10}{3} = 3\frac{1}{3}$$

To change a mixed number ($2\frac{5}{8}$) to an improper fraction, multiply the whole number (2) by the fraction denominator (8). Then add the numerator (5).

$$2\frac{5}{8} = \frac{(2 \times 8) + 5}{8} = \frac{21}{8}$$

To change an improper fraction to a mixed number, divide the numerator by the denominator. Write the remainder over the original denominator.

$$\frac{21}{8} = 8\overline{)21} = 2\frac{5}{8}$$
$$\phantom{\frac{21}{8} = 8} \underline{-16}$$
$$\phantom{\frac{21}{8} = 8 \overline{)2}} 5$$

EQUAL, LIKE, AND UNLIKE FRACTIONS

Fractions are equal, or **equivalent**, when they describe the same part of a region or set. The fractions $\frac{1}{2}$, $\frac{2}{4}$, and $\frac{3}{6}$ are equal.

To reduce a fraction to its **lowest term**, divide the numerator and the denominator by the largest number each part is equally divisible by.

$$\frac{2}{6} \div \frac{2}{2} = \frac{1}{3}$$

When fractions have the same number in their denominators, they are called **like fractions**. These like fractions have a **common denominator** of 5.

$$\frac{3}{5} \text{ and } \frac{2}{5}$$

like fractions

When fractions do not have common denominators, they are **unlike fractions**.

$$\frac{1}{3} \text{ and } \frac{3}{5}$$

unlike fractions

$\frac{9}{9}$ is equal to 1, so it is not a mixed number.

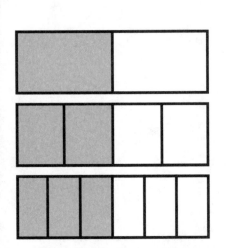

What other fractions are equal to $\frac{1}{2}$? Write your answers on the flap.

FINDING A COMMON DENOMINATOR

- Change unlike fractions ($\frac{1}{3}$ and $\frac{3}{5}$) to like fractions by finding a common denominator of the two fractions.

- Multiply the denominators ($3 \times 5 = 15$). 15 is the new common denominator.

- To find the new numerators, first divide the new denominator by the old denominator.

$$3\overline{)15} = 5 \qquad 5\overline{)15} = 3$$

- Then multiply these answers by the old numerators.

$$\begin{array}{r} 5 \\ \times 1 \\ \hline 5 \end{array} \qquad \begin{array}{r} 3 \\ \times 3 \\ \hline 9 \end{array}$$

The new like fractions are: $\frac{5}{15}$ and $\frac{9}{15}$.

ADDING AND SUBTRACTING FRACTIONS

If fractions are going to be added they must have common denominators. When the denominators are the same, just add the numerators. If the sum is an improper fraction, change it to a mixed number.

$$\frac{3}{4} + \frac{2}{4} = \frac{5}{4} = 1\frac{1}{4}$$

To subtract fractions, first find the least common denominator. Then subtract the numerators. The denominators stay the same.

$$\frac{5}{6} - \frac{2}{3} = ? \quad (\text{LCD is 6}; \ \frac{5}{6} - \frac{4}{6} = \frac{1}{6})$$

To add or subtract mixed numbers, first write them as improper fractions, then perform the required operations.

$$3\frac{2}{3} + 2\frac{1}{3} = \frac{11}{3} + \frac{7}{3} = \frac{18}{3} = 6$$

If the denominators of mixed numbers differ, first, change the numbers to improper fractions, then change unlike fractions to like fractions, and then subtract. If the answer is an improper fraction, change it to a mixed number. (In this example, the LCD is 12.)

$$4\frac{3}{4} - 1\frac{1}{3} = \frac{19}{4} - \frac{4}{3} = \frac{57}{12} - \frac{16}{12} = \frac{41}{12} = 3\frac{5}{12}$$

Solve the following problems.

A. $6\frac{1}{2} + 3\frac{7}{8} = ?$

B. $4\frac{6}{7} - 2\frac{1}{8} = ?$

Write your answers on the flap.

23

MULTIPLYING FRACTIONS

To multiply two fractions ($\frac{1}{2} \times \frac{3}{4}$), first multiply the numerators (1 × 3).

The product (3) is the new numerator.

Then multiply the denominators (2 × 4).

That product (8) is the new denominator.

$$\frac{1}{2} \times \frac{3}{4} = \frac{1 \times 3}{2 \times 4} = \frac{3}{8}$$

To multiply a whole number (2) by a fraction ($\frac{3}{4}$), change the whole number to an improper fraction ($\frac{2}{1}$) and multiply as above. Write the answer as a mixed number and reduce the fraction to its lowest possible terms.

$$\frac{3}{4} \times \frac{2}{1} = \frac{6}{4} = 1\frac{2}{4} = 1\frac{1}{2}$$

Change mixed numbers to improper fractions before you multiply them.

$$1\frac{7}{8} \times 1\frac{1}{2} = \frac{15}{8} \times \frac{3}{2} = \frac{15 \times 3}{8 \times 2} = \frac{45}{16} = 2\frac{13}{16}$$

When a numerator and denominator share a common factor, reduce them to their lowest terms.

$$\frac{4}{5} \times \frac{1}{2}$$

$$\frac{\overset{2}{\cancel{4}}}{5} \times \frac{1}{\underset{1}{\cancel{2}}} = \frac{2}{5}$$

A. The numbers 4 and 2 share a common factor of 2.

B. Divide the numerator and the denominator by the common factor.

C. Multiply.

DIVIDING FRACTIONS

To divide one fraction by another, reverse the numerator and denominator in the divisor fraction. This is called **finding the reciprocal**. Then multiply by the reciprocal.

$$\frac{3}{4} \div \frac{1}{5} = \frac{3}{4} \times \frac{5}{1} = \frac{15}{4} = 3\frac{3}{4}$$

To divide a fraction by a whole number, change the whole number to an improper fraction and follow the same procedure as above.

$$\frac{1}{4} \div 2 = \frac{1}{4} \div \frac{2}{1} = \frac{1}{4} \times \frac{1}{2} = \frac{1}{4 \times 2} = \frac{1}{8}$$

To find the reciprocal, reverse the numerator and the denominator. For example $\frac{1}{5}$ becomes $\frac{5}{1}$.

DECIMALS

Decimals are fractions with denominators of 10 or powers of 10 (100, 1,000, 10,000, and so on).

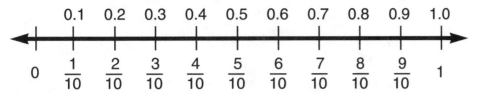

Think of a decimal as a fraction that has the denominator removed and a decimal point placed the same number of places to the left as there are zeroes in the denominator.

$$\frac{75}{100} = 75 \div 100 = 0.75$$

When you write a decimal and a whole number, the decimal point separates the whole number from the fraction.

$$3\frac{1}{100} = 3.01$$

In some decimals, there will be one or more zeroes. Zeroes are placeholders. For example, in 1.001, the zeroes mean there are no tenths and no hundredths and one thousandth.

PLACE-VALUE CHART

A place-value chart can show decimals.

Fraction	Decimal	hundreds 100	tens 10	ones 1	decimal point	tenths 0.1	hundredths 0.01	thousandths 0.001
$614\frac{4}{10}$	614.4	6	1	4	.	4		

Fraction	Decimal	hundreds 100	tens 10	ones 1	decimal point	tenths 0.1	hundredths 0.01	thousandths 0.001
$5\frac{361}{1000}$	5.361			5	.	3	6	1

Fraction	Decimal	hundreds 100	tens 10	ones 1	decimal point	tenths 0.1	hundredths 0.01	thousandths 0.001
$73\frac{9}{100}$	73.09		7	3	.	0	9	

ADDING, SUBTRACTING, MULTIPLYING, DIVIDING DECIMALS

ADDING AND SUBTRACTING DECIMALS

When adding and subtracting decimals, keep the decimal points aligned.

```
        ┌─ align decimal points ─┐
      ↓                          ↓
    21.024                    $79.65
  +145.75                    −34.21
  ────────                   ────────
   166.774                    $45.44
        ↑                          ↑
        └─ align decimal points ─┘
```

MULTIPLYING DECIMALS

Multiply decimals as you would whole numbers.

Count the number of places to the right of the decimal points in the multiplier and the multiplicand and add them.

Count the same number of places from the right of the answer and insert the decimal point.

```
    1
    5.6     one place
  ×  .2     one place
  ──────
  1.12      two places
```

DIVIDING DECIMALS

Divide decimals as you would whole numbers.

$$3.5\,\overline{)\,7}$$

Change the divisor to a whole number. Multiply by a power of 10 to make a whole number.

$$3.5 \times 10 = 35$$

Multiply the dividend by the same power of 10.

$$7 \times 10 = 70$$

Divide.

$$35.\,\overline{)\,70.}\quad\begin{array}{c}2.\end{array}$$

Note that each decimal point has been moved one place to the right and aligned.

Can you multiply these numbers?

.275 × .15 = ?

Write your answer on the flap.

Can you divide these numbers?

A. 5.6)‾1‾1‾2‾ = ?

B. 4.5)‾9‾0‾ = ?

Write your answers on the flap.

CHAPTER 5

Figure It Out

RATIO

A **ratio** is a comparison of two quantities. If your class has 10 boys and 17 girls, the ratio of boys to girls is 10 to 17.

You can write ratios three ways:

$$10 \text{ to } 17 \qquad \frac{10}{17} \qquad 10{:}17 \text{ (read as 10 to 17)}$$

To express ratios, the symbol **:** is usually used to separate the numerator and the denominator.

A **rate** is a ratio that compares two different kinds of units, such as words per minute, miles per hour, or ounces per dollar.

For instance, if 10 ounces of soap cost $2.39 and 25 ounces cost $5.00, divide the price by the quantity to find the cost per ounce.

$$\$2.39 \div 10 = 23.9\cent \text{ per ounce}$$

$$\$5.00 \div 25 = 20\cent \text{ per ounce}$$

Ratios also describe **proportion**. Two ratios that are equal in value are said to be in proportion. To find an equal ratio, you can multiply or divide. Use a fraction equal to 1, such as $\frac{2}{2}$ or $\frac{3}{3}$.

$$5{:}8 \quad \frac{5}{8} \times \frac{3}{3} = \frac{15}{24}$$

5:8 and 15:24 are equal ratios.

$$5{:}8 \quad \frac{5}{8} \div \frac{3}{3} = \frac{15}{24}$$

In a proportion, the cross products of the fractions are equal.

$$5{:}8 = 15{:}24 \quad \text{or} \quad \frac{5}{8} = \frac{15}{24} \qquad (5 \times 24 = 8 \times 15)$$

cross products

$$5 \times 24 = 120$$
$$8 \times 15 = 120$$

WHAT ARE PERCENTAGES?

Percent (%) is a ratio that compares a number with 100. Percent means "per hundred." For example, if 55 out of 100 students said they like school, then 55% of those students like school.

To change a fraction to a percent, divide the fraction.

$$\frac{3}{5} = 5\overline{)3.00}^{.60}$$

Write the decimal as a fraction with a denominator of 100. Then write the percent.

$$.60 = \frac{60}{100} = 60\%$$

To change a percent to a fraction, do the reverse. Be sure to write the fraction in its lowest terms!

$$20\% = \frac{20}{100} = \frac{1}{5}$$

To find a percent of a number (for example, 20% of 60), write the percent in decimal form (.20). Then multiply the decimal by the number.

$$\begin{array}{r} .20 \quad \text{2 places} \\ \times\ 60 \\ \hline 12.00 \quad \text{2 places} \end{array}$$

In other words, 20% of 60 is 12.

USING PERCENT

If boots are 20% off the regular price of $60.00, you can use percent to figure out how much the sale price will be.

$$20\% = .20$$

$$.20 \times \$60 = \$12.00$$

$$\$60.00 - \$12.00 = \$48.00 \ \text{sale price}$$

The sale price of the boots would be $48.00.

If the sales tax is 7.75%, you can use percent to figure out the tax on the boots.

$$7.75\% = .0775$$

$$.0775 \times \$48.00 = \$3.72 \ \text{tax}$$

$$\begin{array}{r} 64 \\ .0775 \quad \text{4 places} \\ \times\ 48.00 \quad \text{2 places} \\ \hline 620000 \\ 3100000 \\ \hline 3.720000 \quad \text{6 places} \end{array}$$

The tax on the boots is $3.72.

To convert a decimal to a percent, move the decimal point two places to the right and add the % sign.

.63 = 63%

To change a percent to a decimal, move the decimal point two places to the left and delete the percent sign.

75% = .75

What would a 15% tip be on a meal that costs $25.49? What would a 20% tip be? Write your answers on the flap.

Measure This

THE CUSTOMARY MEASUREMENT SYSTEM

The United States standard for measurement is called **Customary**, or **English**.

The shortest unit of **length and distance** in the Customary System is the **inch**.

> 1 foot = 12 inches
> 1 yard = three feet (36 inches)
> 1 land mile = 5,280 feet (1,760 yards)

The three customary **scales of weight** in the United States are **avoirdupois** (pounds), **troy** (for weighing gemstones), and **apothecaries' measures** (for weighing medicines).

> **Avoirdupois Weight**
> 1 pound = 16 ounces
> 1 ton = 2,000 pounds

The customary units for measuring **capacity** are **fluid ounces**, **cups**, **pints**, **quarts**, and **gallons**.

> 1 cup = 8 fluid ounces
> 1 pint (16 fluid ounces) = 2 cups
> 1 quart (4 cups) = 2 pints
> 1 gallon (8 pints) = 4 quarts

THE METRIC SYSTEM

The metric system is based on a **meter**, which is one ten-millionth the distance between the North Pole and the Equator. Some common metric prefixes include:

> **milli** – thousand
> **centi** – hundred
> **kilo** – thousand

Equivalents in the metric system are based on tens.

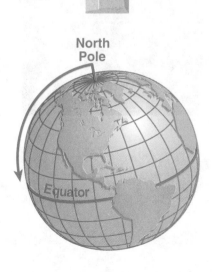

North Pole

Equator

The basic unit of length is the **meter**.

> millimeter = .1 centimeter
> centimeter = 10 millimeters
> meter = 100 centimeters
> kilometer = 1,000 meters

To convert kilometers to miles, multiply kilometers by .62. How many miles equal 4 kilometers? Write your answer on the flap.

A centimeter = the width of an index finger.

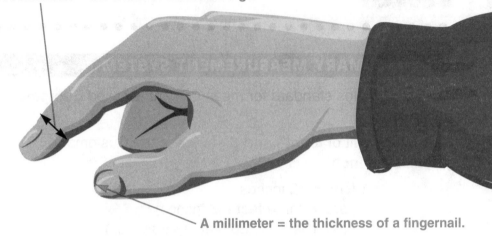

A millimeter = the thickness of a fingernail.

The basic unit of mass in the metric system is the **gram**.

> milligram = .001 gram
> gram = 1,000 milligrams
> kilogram = 1,000 grams
> metric ton = 1,000 kilograms

The basic unit for measuring **capacity** is a **liter**, a term often seen on bottles.

> 10 milliliters = 1 centiliter
> 10 centiliters = 1 deciliter (100 milliliters)
> 1 liter = 10 deciliters (100 centiliters)

Using an inch and centimeter ruler, measure the lines at the right to the nearest inch and the nearest centimeter. Write your answers on the flap.

METRIC CONVERSIONS

1 centimeter = .4 inch

1 kilometer = .62 mile

1 kilogram = 2.2 pounds

1 liter = 33.8 oz. (1 quart + 1.8 oz.)

TEMPERATURE

The **Fahrenheit** and **Centigrade** (or **Celsius**) scales are the two systems for measuring temperature. Both are based on the boiling and freezing points of water.

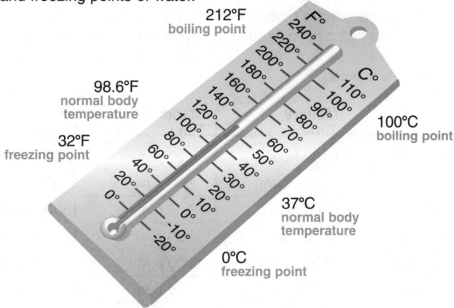

212°F
boiling point

98.6°F
normal body
temperature

32°F
freezing point

100°C
boiling point

37°C
normal body
temperature

0°C
freezing point

To convert Fahrenheit to Celsius, subtract 32 degrees and divide that answer by 1.8. To convert Celsius to Fahrenheit, multiply by 1.8 and add 32 degrees to that answer.

TIME

Our method for measuring time uses **astrometry**. One **day** equals the time it takes for the Earth to make one full rotation on its axis. A **year** is the time it takes the Earth to complete one full orbit around the sun.

> 1 year = 12 months (365 days)
> 1 decade = 10 years
> 1 century = 100 years
> 1 millennium = 10 centuries (1,000 years)

CALENDAR

We use a **calendar** to group days into weeks, months, and years. The calendar most commonly used today is called the **Gregorian**, or **solar** calendar. The Hebrew, Hindi, and Muslim calendars are **lunar** calendars because they're based on the phases of the moon.

Our 24-hour day is divided into two 12-hour sections. The **a.m.**, or **ante meridiem**, hours are from midnight to noon. The **p.m.**, or **post meridiem**, hours are from noon to midnight.

If it's 68°F, what's the temperature in Celsius? Write your answer on the flap.

31

MILITARY TIME

An alternative system for keeping track of time, called **military time**, was developed by scientists to avoid the confusion of a.m. and p.m. Military time is based on a 24-hour clock. Beginning at midnight, the hours are numbered 0 through 24. The military equivalent of 2:00 p.m. is 1400 hours (fourteen hundred hours). Airports use this system to avoid confusing a.m. and p.m. arrival and departure times.

Standard Time	Military Time	Standard Time	Military Time
1:00 a.m.	0100 hours	1:00 p.m.	1300 hours
2:00 a.m.	0200 hours	2:00 p.m.	1400 hours
3:00 a.m.	0300 hours	3:00 p.m.	1500 hours
4:00 a.m.	0400 hours	4:00 p.m.	1600 hours
5:00 a.m.	0500 hours	5:00 p.m.	1700 hours
6:00 a.m.	0600 hours	6:00 p.m.	1800 hours
7:00 a.m.	0700 hours	7:00 p.m.	1900 hours
8:00 a.m.	0800 hours	8:00 p.m.	2000 hours
9:00 a.m.	0900 hours	9:00 p.m.	2100 hours
10:00 a.m.	1000 hours	10:00 p.m.	2200 hours
11:00 a.m.	1100 hours	11:00 p.m.	2300 hours
12:00 noon	1200 hours	12:00 midnight	2400 hours

In military time, 2:30 p.m. would be written as 1430 hours. How would you write 8:45 p.m.? Write your answer on the flap.

UNITS OF MEASURE IN COMPUTERS

In computer processing and storage, the smallest unit of information is called a **bit** (short for binary digit). Information capacity is measured in **bytes**. A byte usually represents one character.

1 bit = 1 binary digit
1 byte = 8 bits
1 kilobyte = 1,000 bytes
1 megabyte = 1 million bytes
1 floppy disc = 1.4 megabytes
1 gigabyte = 1,000 megabytes

CHAPTER 7

Follow That Line: Geometry

The study of points, lines, planes, and shapes is called geometry.

LINES AND POINTS

Lines can go in any direction without end. Points are used to mark where parts of lines begin or end. Points are usually designated by capital letters. Line segments are parts of lines marked by two endpoints.

Lines and line segments are both named by their points. A line is indicated by a straight line with arrows at either end above the letters: $\overleftrightarrow{AB}$. A segment is indicated by a simple straight line above the letters. The part of the line between A and B above is line segment AB: $\overline{AB}$. It can also be called $\overline{BA}$.

Rays, which also are parts of lines, extend in one direction from an endpoint. The symbol for a ray is a straight line with an arrow above the letters naming the ray: $\overrightarrow{AB}$.

Parallel lines extend beside each other, always remaining the same distance apart and never touching or intersecting. The symbol for parallel lines (‖) is read "is parallel to." Line AB is parallel to line CD: $\overleftrightarrow{AB} \parallel \overleftrightarrow{CD}$.

Intersecting lines meet and cross each other at a particular point: $\overleftrightarrow{AB}$ **intersects** $\overleftrightarrow{CD}$ **at point E.**

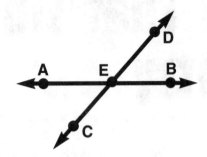

Perpendicular lines form right angles where they intersect. The symbol for perpendicular (⊥) is read "is perpendicular to." Line AB is perpendicular to line CD: $\overleftrightarrow{AB} \perp \overleftrightarrow{CD}$.

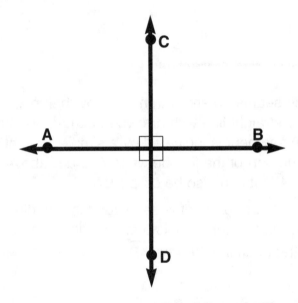

Planes are formed by an infinite set of points on a flat surface. A plane extends infinitely in all directions: **Plane ABCD.**

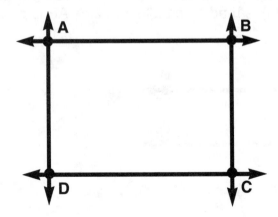

ANGLES

Angles are formed by two rays joined with one endpoint called a **vertex**. The symbol for an angle is ∠ . An angle is named by writing the letters for three points on the lines after the symbol. The middle point names the vertex: ∠ **XYZ.**

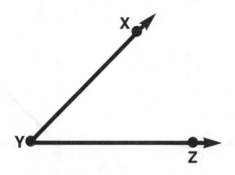

Angles are measured in **degrees** (°) with a **protractor**, a type of ruler marked with degrees.

To draw an angle of a particular size:

• Draw a ray. Label the vertex and a point along the ray (for example, A and B).

• Place the center arrow of the protractor at point A, the vertex, and the zero edge on the ray AB.

• Follow the scale that starts at zero. Mark C at the degree you want your angle.

• Draw a second ray from point A through point C.

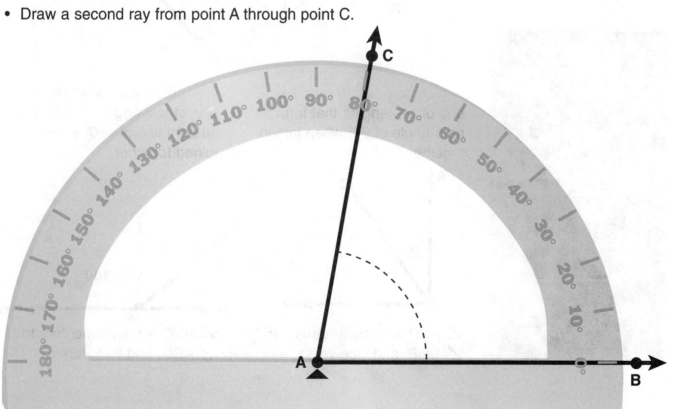

TYPES OF ANGLES

Angles are named according to whether they are less than or more than 90°, 180°, or 360°.

A **right angle** measures exactly 90°.

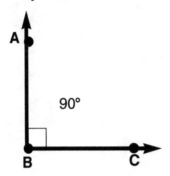

An **acute angle** measures less than 90°.

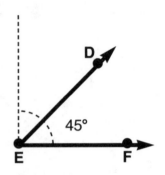

An **obtuse angle** measures more than 90° and less than 180°.

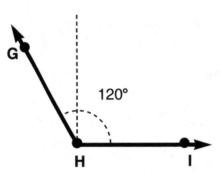

A **reflex angle** measures more than 180°, but less than 360°.

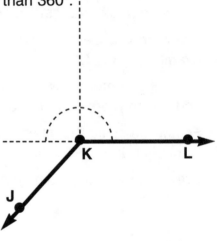

A **complementary angle** is one of two angles that form a right angle of 90° when joined together.

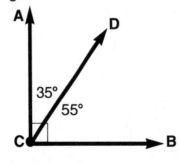

∠ ACD is complementary to ∠ DCB, and vice versa.

A **supplementary angle** is one of two angles that form a straight line of 180° when joined together.

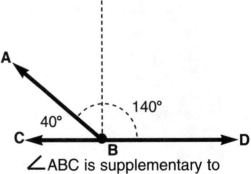

∠ABC is supplementary to ∠ABD, and vice versa.

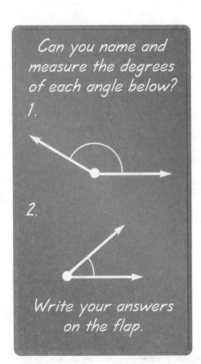

Can you name and measure the degrees of each angle below?

1.

2.

Write your answers on the flap.

CHAPTER 8

Go Figure: Geometric Shapes

POLYGONS

Polygons are flat shapes made of line segments within a single plane. The line segments, which form angles, meet at points called **vertices**.

Irregular polygons, which come in different shapes and sizes, have unequal sides and unequal angles.

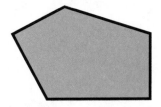 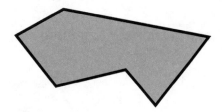

Regular polygons have sides of equal length and angles of equal size.

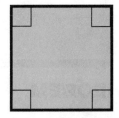 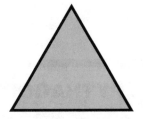

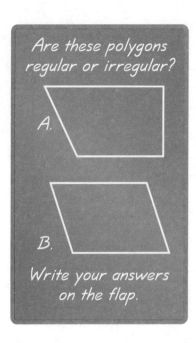

Are these polygons regular or irregular?

A.

B.

Write your answers on the flap.

TRIANGLES

Triangles can be either regular or irregular polygons. They have three sides and three vertices.

In a **right triangle**, two of the three line segments, or **legs**, meet in a 90° angle. The longest side, which connects the two legs, is the **hypotenuse**.

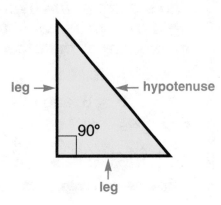

leg → ← hypotenuse

90°

leg

An **isosceles triangle** has two sides the same length.

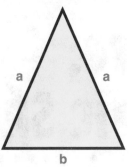

A **scalene triangle** has no sides of equal length.

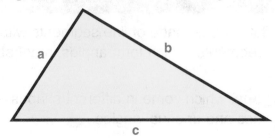

An **equilateral triangle** has three sides of equal length.

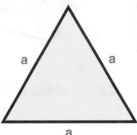

THE PYTHAGOREAN THEOREM

About 2,500 years ago, a Greek philosopher and mathematician named Pythagoras developed the following theorem:

The square of the hypotenuse of a right triangle is equal to the sum of the square of the other two sides.

$a^2 + b^2 = c^2$

If $a = 6$, $b = 8$, and $c = 10$, then

$6^2 + 8^2 = 10^2$

$36 + 64 = 100$

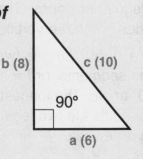

QUADRILATERALS

Quadrilaterals are polygons with four sides and four vertices.

A **parallelogram** is a quadrilateral in which both pairs of opposite sides are parallel line segments. Opposite sides are also equal in length.

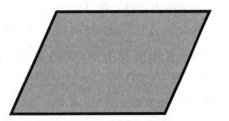

A **rectangle** is a parallelogram with line segments that meet at right angles. There are always four right angles in a rectangle. Each pair of parallel sides has line segments of equal length.

A **square** is a parallelogram with four right angles and all four sides of equal length.

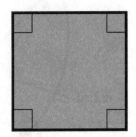

A **rhombus** is a parallelogram with all four sides of equal length but no right angles.

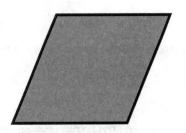

A line drawn inside a polygon from one vertex, or angle, to its opposite vertex is called a diagonal.

A **trapezoid** is a quadrilateral that has only one pair of parallel line segments and no right angles.

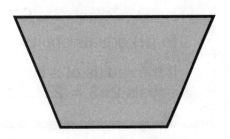

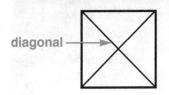

diagonal

CIRCLES

A **circle** is a set of points on a closed plane curve. It has no sides or vertices. Each point on the curve of a circle is equidistant from the **center** point. The curve of a circle between any two points is an **arc**. A full circle has 360°. A half circle, or **semicircle**, has 180°.

The **radius** (r = radius) is the distance from the center point to any point on the boundary of a circle.

The distance around the boundary of a circle is called the **circumference**.

A line drawn through the center of a circle to connect opposite points on the circumference is called the **diameter**. The diameter equals two times the radius (d = 2r).

A **chord** connects any two points on a circle that do not intersect the center.

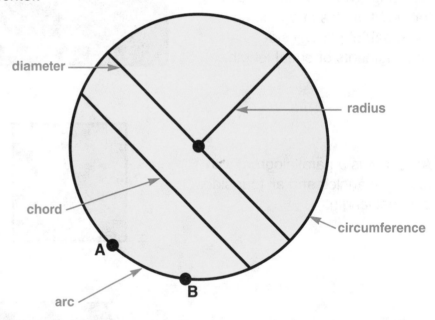

diameter — radius — chord — circumference — A — B — arc

THE FORMULA FOR FINDING THE CIRCUMFERENCE OF A CIRCLE

circumference = two times pi times radius or pi times diameter.

$$c = 2\pi r \text{ or } \pi d.$$

Pi (π) equals approximately 3.14.

If the radius of a circle is 3, the circumference equals $2\pi3 = 2 \times 3.14 \times 3 = 18.84$.

Find the circumference of a circle with a radius of 4. Write your answer on the flap.

SYMMETRY

A fold that equally divides a shape in half is called the **axis**, or **line of symmetry**. A shape can have many lines of symmetry or no lines of symmetry.

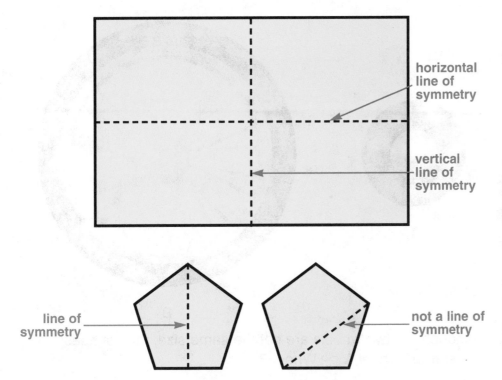

horizontal line of symmetry

vertical line of symmetry

line of symmetry

not a line of symmetry

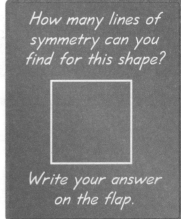

How many lines of symmetry can you find for this shape?

Write your answer on the flap.

CONGRUENCE

Things that are exactly the same size and shape are **congruent**. The symbol for congruence is ≅ and is read "is congruent to."

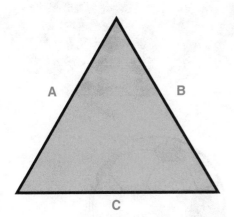

A B

C

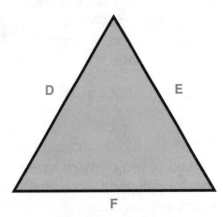

D E

F

△ ABC ≅ △ DEF.

41

SIMILARITY

Shapes that look alike but are not the same size are **similar**. For shapes to be similar, their corresponding angles or degrees of arc must be congruent, and the corresponding sides or curves must be in proportion. The symbol for similar is ∾.

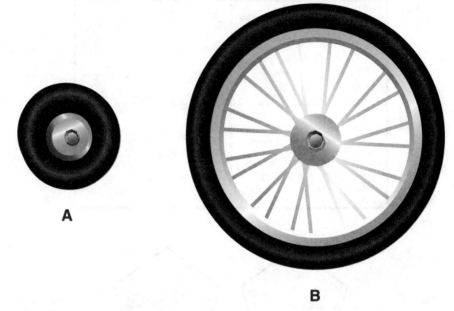

A

B

Congruent shapes are always similar, but similar shapes are not always congruent.

Although the two wheels are not the same size, their shapes are similar. Wheel A ∾ Wheel B.

TESSELATIONS

Shapes can be repeated over a plane to create an interesting design called a **tesselation**. An example of a **pure** and **regular** tesselation is a chess board. One shape, which is a regular polygon, is used to tile the plane.

A **semiregular tesselation** is formed of two or more types of regular polygons. An example of a semiregular tesselation is the design on a soccer ball, which is made up of hexagons and pentagons.

GEOMETRIC SOLIDS

Shapes in three dimensions are called solid or space shapes. Solid shapes have length and width like plane shapes, but they also have a third dimension of height or depth. Cubes, prisms, pyramids, spheres, cones, and cylinders are space shapes.

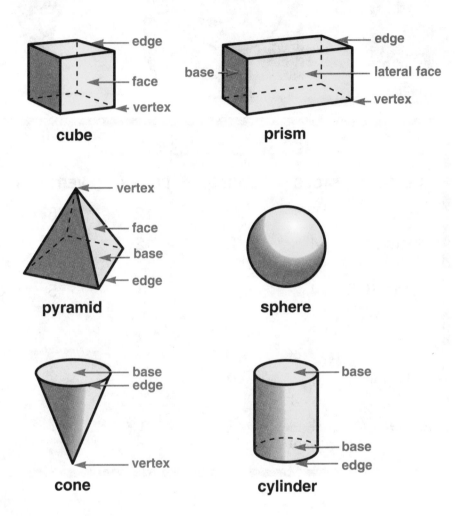

The sides of solids are called faces. A face of a solid is a flat surface in the shape of a polygon. The six faces of a cube are squares. Prisms have two faces called bases that are parallel and congruent. The sides, or lateral faces, are all parallelograms. In pyramids and prisms, the bases can be in the shape of any polygon. In pyramids, all other faces form triangles. The two bases of a cylinder are circles, as is the one base of a cone.

The edges, where faces meet, are similar to line segments. When edges meet, they form a vertex, or corner. Vertices are like points in plane shapes. Prisms, cubes, pyramids, and cones have edges and vertices. Cylinders have edges, but no vertices. A sphere has no vertices, edges, or flat faces.

GEOMETRIC SOLIDS

cylinder

prism

cone

SOLID STATISTICS

SHAPE	FACES	BASES	EDGES	VERTICES
cube	6		12	8
prism (rectangular base)	4	2	12	8
pyramid (rectangular base)	4	1	8	5
sphere	1 (curved)			
cylinder	1 (curved)	2	2	
cone	1 (curved)	1	1	1

Identify the shapes as congruent and/or similar. Write your answers on the flap.

What kind of shape will the figure at the left form if folded? Trace the figure on paper, cut it out along the solid lines, and fold it on the dotted lines to find out.

A.
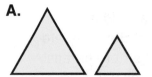

B.
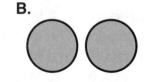

C.
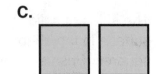

D.
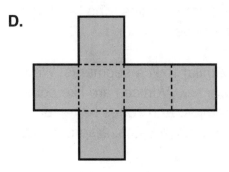

CHAPTER 9

All the Way Around

PERIMETER

PERIMETER

When you measure the outside of a polygon, you are measuring the **perimeter**. Calculating perimeter depends on the shape being measured.

> *To find the perimeter of a polygon with sides that are not of equal length, measure each side, and then add them together.*

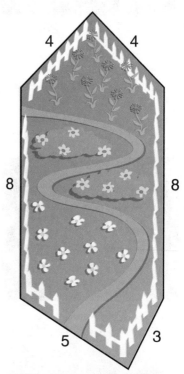

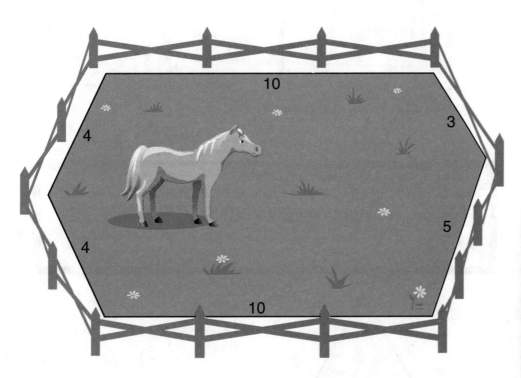

$$10 + 4 + 4 + 10 + 3 + 5 = 36$$

The garden above is shaped like an irregular polygon with sides of 8, 4, 4, 8, 5, 3. What is the perimeter? Write your answer on the flap.

45

PERIMETER

To find the perimeter (P) of a square, multiply the length of one side (s) by 4.

$$s \times 4 = P$$

Find the perimeter of a square with sides that are 3.5 long. Write your answer on the flap.

6

6   6

6

$6 \times 4 = 24$

To find the perimeter (P) of a rectangle, multiply the length (l) by two, and the width (w) by two, then add the totals together.

$$2 \times l + 2 \times w = P$$

Find the perimeter of a rectangle that has a length of 11 and a width of 8. Write your answer on the flap.

6

4   4

6

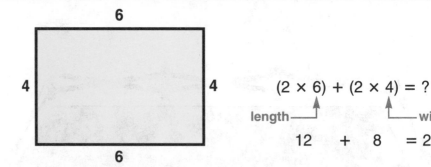

$(2 \times 6) + (2 \times 4) = ?$

length   width

12   +   8   = 20

To find the perimeter (P) of an equilateral triangle, multiply one side (s) by 3.

$$s \times 3 = P$$

Find the perimeter of a triangle that has equal sides of 7. Write your answer on the flap.

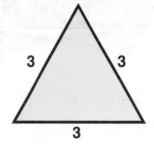

3   3

3

$3 \times 3 = 9$

To find the perimeter (P) of a regular octagon, multiply the length of a side (s) by 8, the number of sides.

s × 8 = P

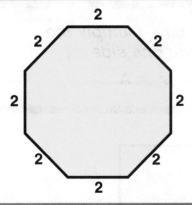

2 x 8 = 16

Find the perimeter of an octagon with sides of 6.5. Write your answer on the flap.

CIRCUMFERENCE

Since there are no sides on a circle to measure, you have to use one of two special equations to find the **circumference** (C), or distance around a circle. To use these equations, you need to know the following:

The **diameter** of a circle (d) is the length of a line drawn through the center point of a circle and connecting two points on the circle.

The **radius** (r) is half of the diameter.

Pi stands for a number that is approximately 3.14. The symbol for pi, which is the sixteenth letter of the Greek alphabet, is π.

C = πd
(circumference equals pi times diameter)
or
C = 2πr
(circumference equals two times pi times radius)

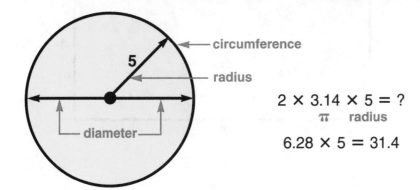

2 × 3.14 × 5 = ?
  π   radius

6.28 × 5 = 31.4

Find the circumference of a circle with a diameter of 11. Write your answer on the flap.

AREA

Area is all of the region inside a plane figure. It is found by measuring the square units within the region, usually the length and width. Equations to find area are based on the shape of the figure being measured.

> **To find the area (A) of a square, multiply the length of two sides or square one side (s).**
>
> $$s \times s = A \ \ or \ \ s^2 = A$$

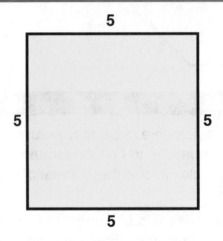

$5 \times 5 = 25 \ \ or \ \ 5^2 = 25$

> Find the area of a square with a side marked 14. Write your answer on the flap.

> **To find the area (A) of a rectangle, multiply the length (l) times the width (w).**
>
> $$l \times w = A$$

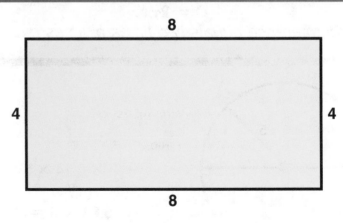

$8 \times 4 = 32$

> Find the perimeter and area of a rectangle with sides marked 7, 7, 3, 3. Write your answer on the flap.

To find the area (A) of a right triangle, multiply the base (b) times the height (h), and divide by 2.

$$\frac{b \times h}{2} = A$$

$$\frac{5 \times 4}{2} = \frac{20}{2} = 10$$

h = 4

90°

b = 5

To find the area (A) of a rhombus, multiply the base (b) times the height (h).

$$b \times h = A$$

4 × 4 = 16

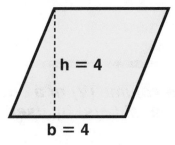

h = 4

b = 4

Find the area of a rhombus with a base of 16 and a height of 12. Write your answer on the flap.

To find the area (A) of a circle, multiply pi times the radius (r) squared.

$$\pi r^2 = A$$

$3.14 \times 6^2 = 3.14 \times 36 = 113.04$

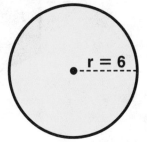

r = 6

Find the area of a circle with a radius of 11. Write your answer on the flap.

VOLUME

The space within a three-dimensional shape is the **volume**. To find volume, measure *length*, *width*, and *height*.

> **The find the volume (V) of a rectangular prism, multiply the length (l) by the width (w) by the height (h).**
>
> $$l \times w \times h = V$$

Find the volume of a rectangular prism with l=10, w=8, h=6. Write your answer on the flap.

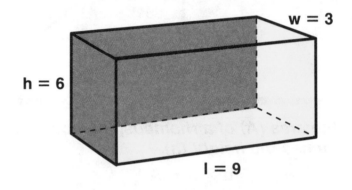

w = 3
h = 6
l = 9

$$9 \times 3 \times 6 = 162$$

> **To find the volume (V) of a cube, multiply the length of one side (s) by itself three times.**
>
> $$s^3 = V$$

Find the volume of a cube having sides that equal 9. Write your answer on the flap.

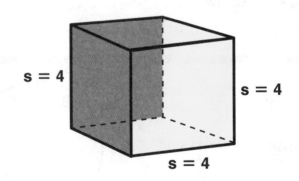

s = 4
s = 4
s = 4

$$4^3 = 4 \times 4 \times 4 = 64$$

To find the volume (V) of a rectangular-base pyramid, multiply the area of the base (b) by the height (h) and divide by 3.

$$\frac{\text{area of b} \times h}{3} = V$$

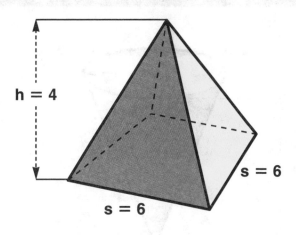

h = 4

s = 6

s = 6

$$\frac{6^2 \times 4}{3} = \frac{36 \times 4}{3} = \frac{144}{3} = 48$$

Since the base of this pyramid is a square, multiply the length of the two sides to find the area.

Calculate the volume (V) of a cylinder by multiplying the area of the base (b) by the height (h). Since the base of a cylinder is a circle, use the formula πr^2 to find the area.

area of b × h = V *or* $\pi r^2 \times h = V$

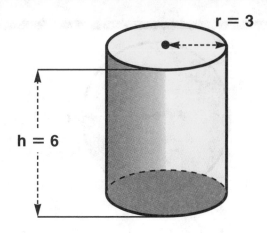

r = 3

h = 6

$3.14 \times 3^2 \times 6 = 3.14 \times 9 \times 6 = 169.56$

Find the volume of a cylinder with a radius of 5 and height of 9. Write your answer on the flap.

51

VOLUME

Calculate the volume (V) of a cone by multiplying the area of the base (b) by the height (h) of the cone and dividing by 3. Since the base of a cone is a circle, use the formula πr² to find the area.

$$\frac{\text{area of b} \times h}{3} = V \text{ or } \frac{\pi r^2 \times h}{3} = V$$

Find the volume of a cone with a height of 8 and a radius of 4. Write your answer on the flap.

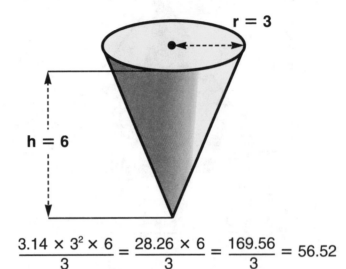

$$\frac{3.14 \times 3^2 \times 6}{3} = \frac{28.26 \times 6}{3} = \frac{169.56}{3} = 56.52$$

To find the volume (V) of a sphere, multiply pi by the radius (r) cubed. Then multiply the product by $\frac{4}{3}$.

$$\pi r^3 \times \frac{4}{3} = V$$

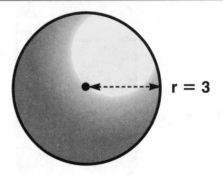

$$3.14 \times 3^3 \times \frac{4}{3} = 3.14 \times 27 \times \frac{4}{3} = 84.78 \times \frac{4}{3} = 113.04$$

CHAPTER 10

Graphs Galore

STATISTICS

Statistics is the branch of mathematics that deals with collecting, organizing, and analyzing numbers. The groups of numbers compared in statistics are called **data**. Data is often presented in a chart or table.

The data in a statistical table can be evaluated as follows:

TERM	DEFINITION
Range	The difference between the lowest and highest number.
Mode	The number that occurs most often in a list. There may be more than one mode.
Median	The middle number when numbers are arranged in order.
Mean	The average of the numbers. (To find the average, add the numbers in the list together, then divide that sum by the number of items.)

MATH TEST SCORES

Student Name	Score
Anna	85
Beth	90
Carson	72
James	85
Jasmine	78
Leroy	94
Maria	97
Reuben	68
Tasha	85
Walt	72

In the "Math Test Scores" table at the left:

What is the range?
What is the mode?
What is the median?
What is the mean?

Write your answers on the flap.

GRAPHS

Graphs are diagrams that show data and are often organized on grids. The data, usually in the form of numbers, is entered on the vertical axis. Items being compared are listed along the horizontal axis.

A bar graph (also called a bar chart) is used to compare data.

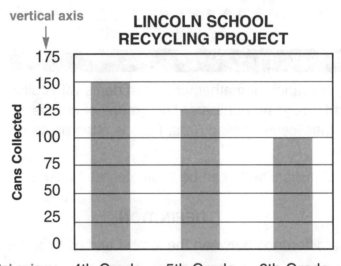

How many cans did the 5th grade collect? Which grade collected the most? Write your answers on the flap.

To find how many cans each grade collected, look across from the top of the bar to the numbers on the vertical axis.

A line graph shows gradual changes in data. A double line graph can be used to compare sets of data.

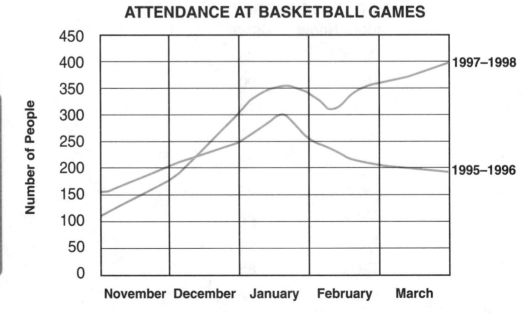

ATTENDANCE AT BASKETBALL GAMES

What month and year had the greatest attendance? What month and year had the lowest attendance? Write your answers on the flap.

A **pictograph** uses little pictures called icons to display and compare data.

To find out what the icons mean or how many numbers each one represents, look at the key below the pictograph.

SUMMER READING

Grade	Books Read	Books Read
4	📘📘📘📘📘📘	?
5	📘📘📘📘📘📘📘	?
6	📘📘📘📘	?

KEY: Each 📘 = 10 books

How many books did each grade read? How many more books did grade 5 read than grade 4? Write your answers on the flap.

A **circle graph** or **pie chart** shows different segments of a group of data in proportion to one another.

MARK'S MONTHLY BUDGET ($100)

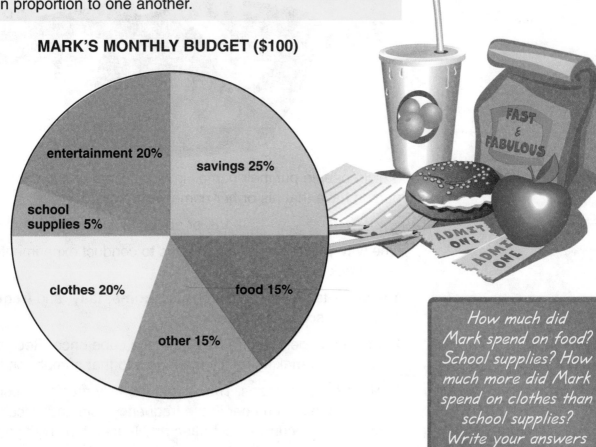

entertainment 20%

savings 25%

school supplies 5%

clothes 20%

food 15%

other 15%

How much did Mark spend on food? School supplies? How much more did Mark spend on clothes than school supplies? Write your answers on the flap.

PROBABILITY

Probability is the likelihood that something will happen. In math, a number is used to describe this. Zero chance means it's impossible something will happen. One chance, however, means something definitely will happen. When the number is between 1 and zero, the chances are said to be unlikely, likely, or very likely that something will happen. For example, if you've ever flipped a coin, you know your chances are 1 out of 2, or 50%, that you'll get either heads or tails. Your chance is greater than zero—because you definitely will get one or the other—but because the result is uncertain, the chances are still less than one.

If eight people put their names in a hat, what chance does each person have that his or her name will be drawn?

1:8, or about 13%

One way you can test probability is to conduct experiments and keep track of the outcomes.

1. Make a table with 3 columns: outcome, tally, and frequency. Number six horizontal rows 1–6.

2. Use a number cube (a die). Toss the cube once. Record the number by making a tally mark next to that number on the table.

3. Make several tosses. Then count the tally marks. Record the totals for each number in the frequency column. Calculate what outcomes occurred most often and least often. Try to make some conclusions about your outcomes.

Now design your own experiment and record your outcomes.

CHAPTER 11

What's the Problem? Word Problems

Often you will be asked to solve math problems that are in the form of short stories. To solve word problems, you need to know what kind of information to look for.

CLUE WORDS

One of the first things you need to do after reading through the problem once is to look for clue words. These are words that will help you identify what mathematical operation you are being asked to perform. Here are some examples:

MATHEMATICAL CLUE WORDS

Addition	Subtraction	Multiplication	Division
add	are left	doubled	as much
all together	change	how many	cut up
both	decreased by	multiplied	divided by
how many	difference	product of	equal groups
in all	fewer	times	half
increased by	how much		parts
plus	less than		quotient of
sum	remain		separated
together	subtract		sharing equally
total	take away		split

SIMPLIFYING THE PROBLEM

After identifying clue words, find the numerical information you need. Write it down or circle it. Cross out the rest.

If an elephant runs 36.6 feet per second and a cheetah runs 102 feet per second, how much farther can a cheetah run in one second than an elephant?

CLUE WORDS: how much

Numerical Information:

elephant–36.6 feet per second

cheetah–102 feet per second

Mathematical Operation: subtraction

$$102.0 - 36.6 = 65.4$$

65.4 In one second the cheetah runs 65.4 feet farther than an elephant.

The Youth Center plans a picnic for 67 people. If each person will drink 3 sodas and eat 2 hamburgers, how many sodas and burgers does the Center need to buy?

CLUE WORDS: how many

Numerical Information:

67 people

3 sodas and 2 hamburgers each

Mathematical Operation: add or multiply

$67 \times 3 = 201$ sodas; $67 \times 2 = 134$ hamburgers

$67 + 67 + 67 = 201$ sodas; $67 + 67 = 134$ hamburgers

SOME COMMON STRATEGIES FOR SOLVING WORD PROBLEMS

- eliminate unnecessary information
- guess and check
- find a pattern
- make and use tables
- make drawings or diagrams
- make a list
- solve a simpler problem
- use logic
- work backward
- write an equation

1. At a party, 4 people shook hands with each other. How many handshakes were made?

   STRATEGY: Make a List

   A, B, C, D represent the 4 people.

   Write down each handshake.

   AB   AC   AD

   BC   BD   CD

   (answer: 6)

2. Cody is 3 inches taller than Brian. Jamal is 3 inches taller than Cody. Cody is $4\frac{1}{2}$ feet tall. How tall are Brian and Jamal?

   STRATEGY: Use Logic

   What You Know: Cody is $4\frac{1}{2}$ feet tall.

   Compare: Brian is 3 inches shorter than Cody.

       4 ft. 6 in. − 3 in. = 4 ft. 3 in.

       Jamal is 3 inches taller than Cody.

       4 ft. 6 in. + 3 in. = 4 ft. 9 in.

Brenda has a choice of black or brown shorts and white, green, or red shirts. How many different outfits can she choose from? Write your answers on the flap.

3. A cafeteria has square tables that seat 4 people. When 2 tables are moved end to end, 6 people can sit. If 3 tables are pushed together, 8 people can sit. How many people can be seated if 10 tables are placed end to end?

   STRATEGY: Find a Pattern

Tables	People
1	4
2	6
3	8
4	10
5	12
6	14
7	16
8	18
9	20
10	22

   (answer: 22 people)

How would you solve this problem?

Roy is drawing a triangular pattern. He draws 1 triangle in the first row. He draws 2 triangles in the second row and 3 triangles in the third row. How many rows can he make if he draws 45 triangles?

Write your answer on the flap.

4. Sam scored 5 points when he hit a target in a video game. He already had 25 points. Then he hit the target 57 times in a row. After his last hit, was Sam's score an odd or an even number?

STRATEGY: Solve a Simpler Problem

What to Do: Find the score for the first few hits.

Hit	Score
1	30
2	35
3	40
4	45

You'll see that for every odd number hit, the score is even. For every even number hit, the score is odd. The number 57 is an odd number, so the score will be even.

5. Rachel bought 30 new software disks for the school. She bought twice as many science disks as she did game disks. There were three times as many word processing disks as there were game disks. How many of each kind of disk were there?

STRATEGY: Guess and Check

What You Know: 30 total disks; twice as many science disks as game disks; 3 times as many word processing disks as game disks.

What to Do: Choose numbers that may add up to 30; the second number must be twice as much as the first; the third number must be 3 times as much as the first:

4 + 8 + 12 = 24 (too low)

Try Again: 5 + 10 + 15 = 30

Rachel bought 5 game disks, 10 science disks, and 15 word processing disks.

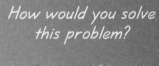

How would you solve this problem?

Jennifer put 20 tables and chairs in the meeting room. She brought in 4 times as many chairs as tables. How many of each did she bring in to the room?

Write your answer on the flap.

PAGE 5
2 and 1 are the factors;
prime numbers from 51 to 100:
53, 59, 61, 67, 71, 73, 79, 83,
89, 97

PAGE 6
Composite numbers from 51 to
100: 51, 52, 54, 55, 56, 57, 58,
60, 62, 63, 64, 65, 66, 68, 69,
70, 72, 74, 75, 76, 77, 78, 80,
81, 82, 84, 85, 86, 87, 88, 90,
91, 92, 93, 94, 95, 96, 98, 99,
100

PAGE 7
200,000,000,000 +
20,000,000,000 +
2,000,000,000 + 200,000,000
+ 20,000,000 + 2,000,000 +
200,000 + 20,000 + 2,000 + 200
+ 20 + 2; two hundred twenty-
two billion, two hundred twenty-
two million, two hundred twenty-
two thousand, two hundred
twenty-two

PAGE 8
16 = XVI, 40 = XL, 104 = CIV

PAGE 10
A. 297; **B.** 15,501; **C.** 11,129

PAGE 11
A. 20,000; **B.** 7,000; **C.** 8,000;
D. 20,000

PAGE 12
A. 4; **B.** -4
Magic Square Answers:
top row: 3; third row: 7

PAGE 14
$11.99 x 5 = $59.95;
A. 1,462; **B.** 23,548;
C. 437,076

PAGE 15
two common multiples of 4
and 10: 20, 40; least common
multiple of 6 and 8: 24

PAGE 16
prime factors of 30 are 2, 3, and
5; prime factors of 44 are 2 and
11; $5^4 = 5 \times 5 \times 5 \times 5 = 625$

PAGE 17
47

PAGE 18
A. 1,167 R6; **B.** 767 R2; **C.** 9

PAGE 19
$5 \times 4^3 + 16 + 8$; $5 \times 64 + 16 + 8$;
$320 + 16 + 8$; $336 + 8 = 344$

PAGE 20
19

PAGE 22
Answers may vary. Possible
answers are: $\frac{5}{10}$, $\frac{4}{8}$, and $\frac{6}{12}$

PAGE 23
A. $10\frac{3}{8}$; **B.** $2\frac{41}{56}$

PAGE 26
.275 x .15 = .04125; **A.** 20;
B. 20

PAGE 28
15% tip is $3.82; 20% tip is
$5.10

PAGE 30
2.5 miles; **top line:** 4 inches, or
10 centimeters; **bottom line:** 5
inches, or 12.5 centimeters

PAGE 31
68°F = 20°C

PAGE 32
2045 hours

PAGE 36
160° obtuse angle;
40° acute angle

PAGE 37
A. irregular; **B.** regular

PAGE 40
25.12

PAGE 41
4

PAGE 44
A. similar; **B.** congruent and
similar; **C.** congruent and
similar; **D.** cube

PAGE 45
32

PAGE 46
P of square = 14; P of
rectangle = 38; P of
triangle = 21

PAGE 47
P of octagon = 52;
Circumference = 34.54

PAGE 48
A of square = 196; P of
rectangle = 20, A of
rectangle = 21

PAGE 49
A of rhombus = 192;
A of circle = 379.94

PAGE 50
V of rectangular prism = 480;
V of cube = 729

PAGE 51
V of cylinder = 706.5

PAGE 52
V of cone = 133.97

PAGE 53
range = 29; mode = 85;
median = 85; mean = 82.6

PAGE 54
Gr. 5 collected 125 cans;
Gr. 4 collected the most cans;
March 1998; November 1997

PAGE 55
60, 80, 40; 20; Food—$15.00;
School Supplies—$5.00; $15.00

PAGE 59
6 outfits;
Find a pattern: 9 rows

PAGE 60
Guess and Check: 16 chairs,
4 tables